Art & Activities for Kids

Make Prints!

Kim Solga

Cincinnati, Ohio

Note to Parents and Teachers

The activities in this book were developed for the enjoyment of children. We've taken every precaution to ensure their safety and success. Please follow the directions, and note where an adult's help is required. In fact, feel free to work alongside your young artists as often as you can. They will appreciate help in reading and learning new techniques, and will love the chance to talk and show off their creations. Children thrive on attention and praise, and art adventures are the perfect setting for both.

95 94 93 92   5 4 3 2

Library of Congress Cataloging in Publication Data

Solga, Kim.
    Make prints! / Kim Solga.
        p.   cm.
    Summary: Presents step-by-step instructions for printing colorful impressions using a variety of materials and surfaces.
    ISBN 0-89134-384-9
    1. Prints—Technique—Juvenile literature.   [1. Prints—Technique.]
I. Title.
NE855.S5   1991
760—dc20   90-27851
                                                    CIP
                                                    AC

Edited by Julie Wesling Whaley
Designed by Clare Finney
Photography Direction by Kristi Kane Cullen
Art Production by Suzanne Whitaker
Photography by Pamela Monfort
Very special thanks to Niki Smith, Corey Snyder and Autumn Wright

About This Book (A Note to Grown-Ups)

Make Prints! features eleven unique printing projects plus numerous variations that will fire the imagination of boys and girls aged six to eleven. By inviting kids to try new things, *Make Prints!* encourages individual creativity. Young artists will love doing these activities even while they're learning basic principles of art and printmaking. In traditional projects — as well as some unconventional ones — they'll be printing with found objects from around the house and yard, bars of soap and wood blocks, erasers, melted crayons, silk screens, vegetables, and perhaps the simplest tools of all, their fingers! All the while they'll be exploring patterns and shapes, textures, spontaneous design, and positive and negative space.

Each project has a theme, stated at the very beginning, and some projects suggest follow-up activities related to that theme. Some projects result in beautiful finished works to display or give away; others emphasize experimentation and the simple fun of doing them. They're all kid-tested to ensure success and inspire confidence.

Getting the Most Out of the Projects

Each project is both fun to do and educational. While the projects provide clear step-by-step instructions and photographs, each is open-ended so kids may decide what they want to print. Some of the projects are easy to do in a short amount of time. Others require more patience and even adult supervision. The symbols on page 6 will help you recognize the more challenging activities.

The list of materials shown at the beginning of each activity is for the featured project only. Suggested alternatives may require different supplies. Feel free to substitute! For example, almost all of the projects that call for a brayer and printing ink can also be done with tempera paint and sponge pieces. The projects offer flexibility to make it easy for you and your child to try as many activities as you wish.

Collecting Supplies

All of the projects can be done with household items or inexpensive, easy-to-find supplies (see page 7 for definitions of any art materials you're not already familiar with). Here are some household items you'll want to make sure you have on hand: newspapers, scrap cardboard, an old cookie sheet, old crayons, string, liquid laundry starch, aluminum foil, sponges, paper towels, masking tape.

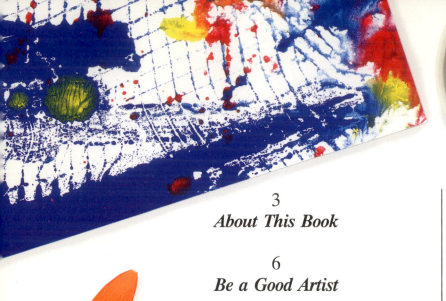

4

Be a Good Artist

Work Habits

Get permission to work at your chosen workspace before you begin. Cover your workspace with newspapers or a vinyl tablecloth.

Wear a smock or old T-shirt to protect your clothes. Wash your hands often as you make prints so you won't get smudges on your paper.

Follow the directions carefully for each project. When you see this symbol, have an adult help you.

Don't put art materials in your mouth. If you're working with a younger child, don't let him put art materials in his mouth, either.

The clock symbol means you must wait to let something dry before going on to the next step. It is very important not to rush ahead.

Finish by cleaning your workspace and all of your tools. Wash brushes in warm water until the water runs clear, and store with bristles up.

Get Ready

Collect things you think will make good prints: leaves, feathers, spools, coins, hardware, and little toys. Make sure they're clean.

You'll create lots of prints. Make a clothesline out of string and plastic clothes-pins so you can hang wet prints to dry.

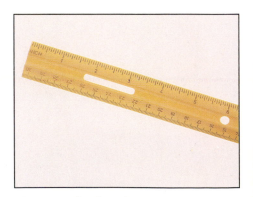

Have a ruler handy so you can measure things. This symbol, ", means inches—12" means 12 inches; cm means centimeters.

Art Materials

Tempera Paint. Also called poster paint, tempera paint is a water-based paint that is opaque—you can't see through it. You can buy it in an art supply store already mixed with water (a liquid paint in a bottle or jar) or as a powder that you can mix yourself with an adult's help.

Water-based Printing Ink. A nontoxic printmaking ink that comes in a tube. It's smooth and very sticky, but it washes off with soap and water.

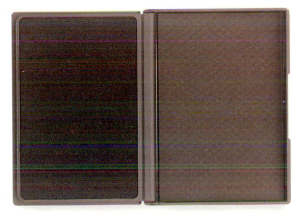

Ink Pads. Ink pads are made for rubber stamps and they come in lots of great colors. Be sure to buy ink pads with nontoxic inks. Sometimes craft stores have fabric ink pads you can use on clothes, and the ink won't wash out.

Printing Paper. You can print on many different kinds of paper. Soft, absorbent paper will pick up the ink and paint best. Use white drawing paper, construction paper, typing paper—even brown paper bags.

Paintbrushes. There are many different kinds of brushes for different uses. You can use a wide brush to spread a thin layer of paint on your printing block if you choose to use paint instead of ink. Use a very thin brush to add details or touch up areas that didn't print well. Use a wide "foam brush" (from the hardware store) to spread paint on big things you want to print with.

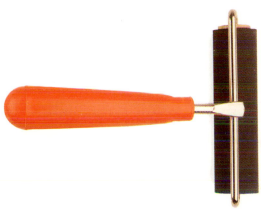

Brayer. A rubber roller used to spread a very thin layer of ink. You hold the brayer by its handle and roll it in ink poured in a shallow dish or pan. Then you roll it on the surface of a printing block (Hammered Wood, Soap Block Prints) or on an object you want to print with (Collections, Nature Prints).

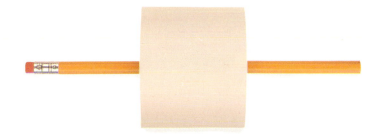

You can make your own brayer! Cover a roll of adding machine paper with clear tape and stick a pencil down the middle for a handle. Hold it like a rolling pin and you're ready to roll!

Collections

Studying Patterns and Shapes

What do clothespins, thread spools, bottle caps and hair curlers have in common? Answer: They all make great Collection Prints.

Materials needed:

Tempera paint (or water-based ink)

Things to print with

White or colored paper

Newspaper or scrap paper

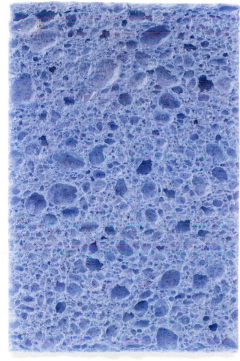

Pieces of sponge (or brayer)

1 Collect things that have interesting shapes. Make sure they can be washed clean or thrown away after you print with them.

2 You'll use several methods to print with the things in your collection. Lay big, flat things like lace on a piece of scrap paper.

3 Use a sponge to pat on paint (or use a brayer to roll ink). Move the painted object onto a piece of clean scrap paper, lay white paper on top and rub.

4 For small, hard objects use sponge pieces, a brayer or your fingers to spread on a thin coat of paint or ink. Then stamp the object down on your white paper.

5 Some things like string or chains can be dipped into a bowl of paint, then laid out carefully on clean scrap paper. Lay your printing paper on top and press.

6 Soft things can be dabbed into paint that's been spread thin on a plate. Pat them into the paint a few times, then stamp them onto your printing paper.

Collecting Fun

Print different things on one sheet of white paper to make a collage. Print the largest things first, then the smaller things on top or next to them. If you use different colors, let each color dry before going on.

Print lots of things on different papers, then cut them out when they're dry. Glue the cut-out prints on another paper to create a design.

Use the things in your collection to build a picture! In this example, a bottle cap is the dog's body, a key makes the man's arms, and a piece of string printed the leash.

Prints Charming

Making a Monoprint

"Mono" is a Latin word meaning one. In this project you'll make one print of each painting you create. It's fun to try different color and texture combinations!

Tempera paint

Materials needed:

Paintbrush

White paper

Liquid laundry starch

Old cookie sheet

1 Pour a little starch onto the cookie sheet. Add one or more colors of paint.

2 Make swirls of color, blend colors together, or drip and splatter dots of paint.

3 Lay a piece of paper on top. Gently rub, then lift the paper to see your print. Wipe the cookie sheet clean and start another!

Charming Monoprints

Place cut or torn pieces of paper and leaves over your painting before you lay the white paper on top. This will block part of the paint and make interesting designs.

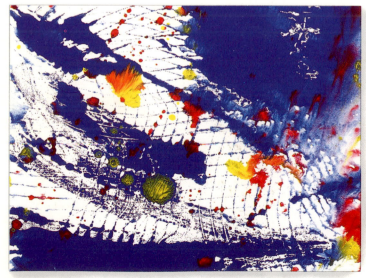

Collect objects to make textures in your painting—drag a comb through it, dab a crumpled piece of aluminum foil on it, or drive a toy car through it!

Add glitter while the paint is wet, and felt pen lines after it's dry. Make a realistic picture if you wish—but keep your subject simple.

Monoprint Drawing

1 Roll a *thin* layer of water-based printing ink onto a cookie sheet with a brayer. Use one color or roll on several colors.

2 Gently lay a piece of white paper on top of the ink. Use a pencil to draw a picture on the paper. Press hard!

3 When you're finished drawing, lift the paper to see your print on the bottom side!

Nature Prints

Seeing Invisible Textures

You can capture the beautiful textures of nature with these fast and simple prints. Leaves, pine needles, feathers, flowers, seaweed and even fish make wonderful designs.

Materials needed:

Cotton

Paintbrushes

Paper towels

Print a Fish

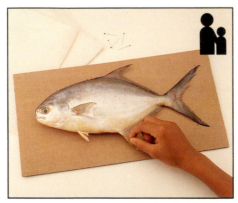

1 Clean your fish with a damp paper towel. If the insides have been removed, stuff it with paper towels so its belly is round and firm.

2 Lay the fish on a piece of cardboard. Spread out the tail and fins and pin them down or prop them up with bits of paper towel.

3 Cover the eye with a little piece of cotton and let your fish dry for two hours before going on.

White paper
Cardboard

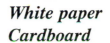

Scrap newspaper

A fish (big and flat, with rough scales and hard fins)

Tempera paint

Straight pins

4 Pull the pins out and slip newspaper under your fish. Brush a layer of thick tempera paint onto the fish.

5 Pull out the newspaper and lay white paper on the painted fish. Carefully rub all over the fish, especially its face, fins and tail.

6 Lift the paper to see your print! After your print is dry, use a thin brush to paint in an eye and touch up areas that didn't print well.

Natural Textures

Brush Prints
Hold a flower or feather on newspaper and brush a layer of tempera paint on top. Set the painted flower or feather on a clean piece of newspaper, paint side up. Lay a piece of white paper on top and rub gently.

Fishy Shirts
Print a fish right onto a T-shirt or sweatshirt. Use fabric paint so the fish won't come out in the wash!

Brayer Prints
Hold a leaf by its stem on a piece of
newspaper. Roll ink all over one side.
Lay the leaf on white paper, ink side
down. Cover with clean newspaper
and rub.

Negative Leaves
Lay a piece of paper on the bottom
of a big box. Place several leaves on
the paper. Dip a toothbrush into
paint, hold it down in the box, and
rub your thumb over the bristles to
splatter the paint. Keep going until
the leaves and paper are covered with
dots.

Symmetrical Prints

Creating Spontaneous Designs

These prints are almost like accidents: You don't plan them out, you just let them happen—and they're beautiful! Because you fold a piece of paper and then unfold it, the design is symmetrical, meaning it's the same on both sides of the fold.

Materials needed:

Rinse water

String

Clothing iron

Tempera paint

White paper and aluminum foil

Knife   **Paintbrushes**

Old, broken crayons

Crayon Melts

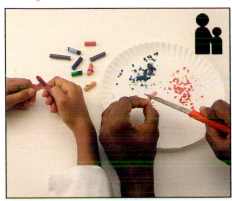

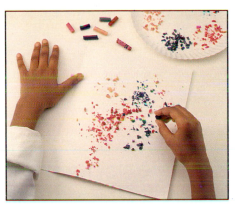

1 Peel the paper off old, broken crayons and have an adult chop them into tiny pieces. Fold a piece of paper in half, then open it.

2 Arrange bits of crayon on one side of the paper to make a design. Carefully fold your paper again, bringing the blank half over on top of the crayon design.

3 Cover the bottom of an iron with foil before turning it on. Have an adult iron the folded paper. Unfold the paper while it's still hot to see the melted design inside.

Double Designs

1 Fold a paper in half, then open it. Brush, drip and splatter paints on one side of the fold. Rinse your brush after each color.

2 When you're done painting, fold the paper, rub gently, then unfold it to see your colorful two-sided print!

String Pulls

1 Fold a paper in half, then open it. Dip an 18″ (45 cm) piece of string into a bowl of paint, holding on to one clean end.

2 Lay the paint-covered string on one side of the paper, looping and curling it around. Fold the paper again and hold it down.

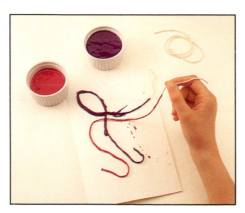

3 Pull the string out and unfold the paper to see your design. Let one color dry, then do another string with a different color.

4 Or, for a different look, set up several painted strings at the same time, fold the paper, and pull them out one by one.

Make an abstract double design with colorful drips and splatters.

Butterflies, flowers, and apples are good subjects for Double Designs.

Make a realistic picture. Paint half the picture on one side of the fold—folding and pressing creates the whole design.

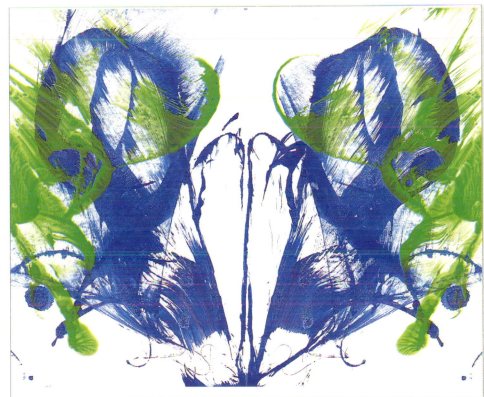

Do many different String Pulls—try pulling fast and pulling slowly. Experiment with thread, yarn, ribbon, jewelry chains.

Hammered Wood

Making a Wood Block

You'll get some exercise as you pound designs into wood with a hammer! Using wood blocks is a very traditional and professional way of printing. Wood blocks make beautiful prints because you can engrave thin lines and interesting patterns in them, and the natural wood grain adds a special look.

Old, weathered wood

Materials needed:

Hammer

Small, flat pieces of pine, balsa, redwood

Pencil

1 Collect pieces of metal with interesting shapes—get permission to use them! Ask an adult to help you if you've never used a hammer before.

2 Hold a metal tool against the wood and hit it with a hammer. Experiment! Some tools need only a soft tap; others need to be pounded hard.

Caution! Work slowly and be very careful not to hurt yourself with the hammer or metal tools. Cover machine parts and gears with a cloth before hammering them.

Brayer

Carbon paper
White paper

Water-based
printing ink

WATER SOLUBLE INK
FOR BLOCK PRINTING
RED

NET CONT. 37cc

Metal tools

Crayon

4 Test your block before printing:
Lay a piece of paper on top and
rub with a crayon to see how your
design will look.

5 When you're happy with your
design, roll a thin layer of ink on
your block. Put a piece of paper on
top and rub hard with your fingers.

6 To print a realistic picture, draw
it on paper first. Use carbon
paper to transfer your sketch onto
the wood and then engrave your
design with metal tools.

Pounded Patterns

If your design has words or numbers in it, make them *backwards* on your block so they'll print the right way.

Tap on the handle of a flat screwdriver to make a little line. Move it just a bit and tap it again, move it and tap, move it and tap, to cut a straight or curved line.

Use different tools to make different patterns. Nails will make little round holes. The end of a bolt can make a square or hexagon.

This coyote was printed with a block made of styrofoam pieces glued onto heavy cardboard.

Styrofoam Blocks

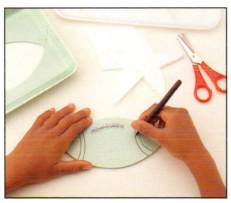

1 Find an old block of styrofoam packing material, or clean off the styrofoam tray from a package of meat or fruit.

2 Cut shapes out of the foam and "carve" or draw designs into it with a ball-point pen. Press hard.

3 When your design is finished, roll on some ink, lay a piece of paper on top, and rub over it with your fingers to make a print.

Fingerprinting

Printing a Story

Make dozens of characters and pictures with tools you always have on hand—your fingers! You can even create your own cartoon strips.

Materials needed:

White paper

Washable ink pad

Felt-tip pen

Tempera paint

1 Make lots of fingerprints by touching the ink with your finger, then pressing it onto the paper. Wash your hands while the fingerprints dry.

2 Using a felt pen, add eyes, smiles, arms and legs, hair and clothes to make people! You can also create animal characters.

3 Have fun creating comic strips! Show motion by drawing lines around your characters. Make them talk or think by adding balloons or bubbles with words in them.

Animal Tracks

Carving a Likeness

Who walked all over the writing paper? Who left their footprints on the birthday presents? Here's how to make fancy designs with the tracks of your favorite animals.

Materials needed:

Ink pad

Hobby knife

Eraser

Felt-tip pens

Paper

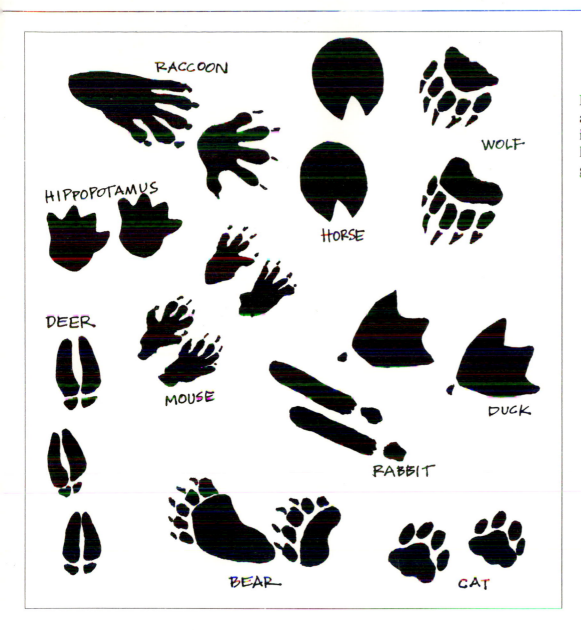

RACCOON

WOLF

HIPPOPOTAMUS

HORSE

DEER

MOUSE

DUCK

RABBIT

BEAR

CAT

Find out what your favorite animal's track looks like. If it isn't shown here, go to the library and ask for a field guide to animal tracks.

1 Make a small drawing of a footprint on one side of an eraser with a felt pen. Keep your drawing very simple.

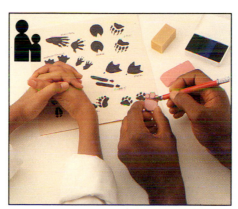

2 Have an adult help you cut *around* your drawing. Carve down at least ¼ inch (½ cm) or carve away the whole eraser.

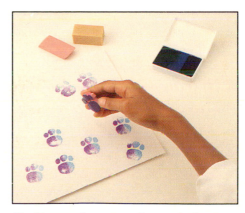

3 Stamp the carved eraser footprint onto the ink pad and press it onto your paper. Check the design and carve more if you need to.

Animal Track Treasures

Carefully stamp blown-up balloons— wow!

Use fabric paints or latex house paints to decorate T-shirts. This track was made with a potato stamp.

Throw a wildlife party! Stamp invitations, gift cards and thank you cards.

Make wrapping paper by stamping shelf paper or newsprint.

Take your animal for a walk across writing paper to make stationery.

Make colorful ink pads!
Fold up pieces of paper towel and drip food coloring on top.

Footprint variations
There's more than one way to make animal tracks. Get permission and have an adult help you with these footprinting projects.

Pet Prints

1 Use *nontoxic* paint to collect prints of gentle pets like your dog or cat. Spread a thin layer of paint on a paper plate.

2 Press the animal's paw into the paint, then onto the paper. Wipe the paw as clean as you can with wet paper towels.

Potato Paws

1 Cut a potato in half and dry it. Draw a footprint onto the cut surface with a felt pen. Have an adult carve all around your track.

2 Dip the stamp into a shallow dish of paint, or paint just the footprint with a paintbrush, and then stamp it.

Rubbings

Working with Textures and Impressions

If you look carefully, you can find interesting textures all around you: in car tires and tennis shoe soles, wood and tile walls and floors, tree bark, wicker and cloth. It's fun to collect these patterns and designs by making rubbings.

Masking tape

Materials needed:

Textured objects

White paper

Dark crayons with the paper peeled off

1 Lay a piece of paper on top of the object you want an impression of. Don't let the paper wiggle — use tape to hold it in place.

2 Rub over the object gently with the side of a crayon. Practice making it lighter or darker until you can really see the bumpy patterns.

3 Try using different colors. You'll see textures in the rubbings that you'd never notice just looking at the objects!

Make an interesting picture with a collection of items: a glove and a shoe, leaves and tree bark, string and coins, or any combination.

Collect textures from all around the house and yard. Divide your paper into squares and fill each square with a different pattern.

Divide your paper into thirty spaces (draw four lines across and five lines up and down). Make rubbings of the alphabet from mailboxes, cars, shoes and signs.

Veggie Geometry

Repetition in Design

Vegetables are good for you—if you're a print-maker! Slice a vegetable or a piece of fruit in half to reveal an interesting design inside. Then use them to print a repeating pattern, or use the shapes to create a picture.

Materials needed:

Tempera paint

Sponge pieces

Fruits or vegetables

Knife *Paintbrush*

White paper

1 Have an adult help you slice each fruit or vegetable smoothly down the middle. Pat it dry with paper towels.

2 Use a paintbrush, sponge pieces or your fingers to cover the sliced surface with paint. Press it onto paper to print.

3 Create a circle design by printing different veggie shapes around the center shape, keeping the pattern the same on each side.

Mixed Vegetables

Print a veggie forest! Draw slanting lines for hills, then print broccoli and cauliflower trees. Build a car, or animal, or any veggie picture—use your imagination!

Make a veggie face, using different vegetables to create eyes, nose, mouth and hair. Or make a beautiful bouquet of flowers.

Soap Block Printmaking

Understanding Positive and Negative Images

You can carve interesting designs into flat bars of soap and use them to print dozens of beautiful pictures.

Materials needed:

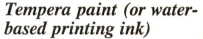

Tempera paint (or water-based printing ink)

Sponge piece (or brayer)

Carrot peeler and masking tape

Carving Your Block

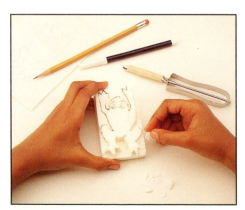

1 Trace the block on a piece of paper and plan a simple design with a pencil. Draw your design on the soap with a felt pen.

2 Use the carrot peeler wrapped with masking tape to carve around your design. Clean off the soap bits and throw them away.

Caution! Always push the carving tool **away** from you. Turn your block when you need to carve in a different direction.

40

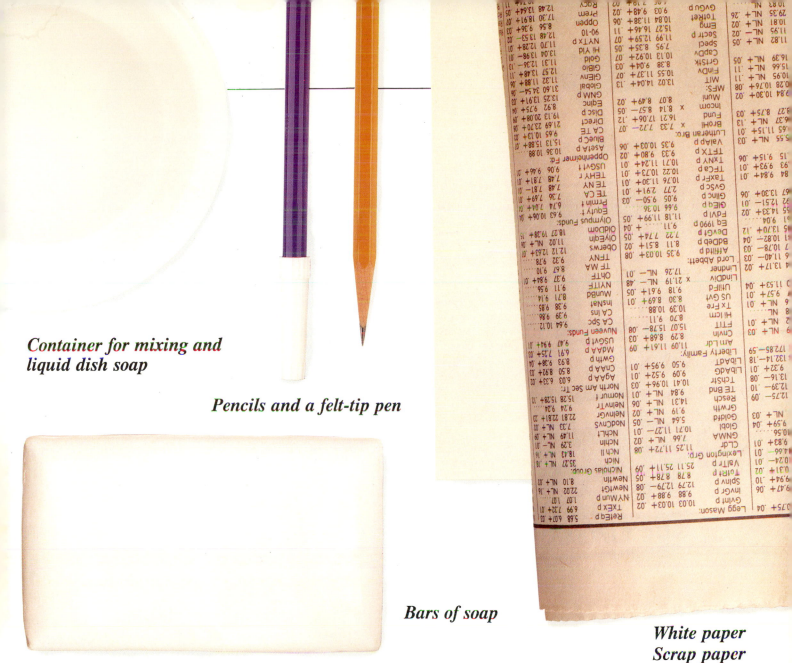

Container for mixing and liquid dish soap

Pencils and a felt-tip pen

Bars of soap

White paper
Scrap paper

Printing Your Block

1 Dip the sponge piece into the paint and pat it onto your carved block. You may need to add a drop of dish soap to the paint.

2 Or, use a brayer to roll on a thin layer of ink. Place the block paint or ink side up on a clean piece of scrap paper.

3 Set a piece of white paper on top, hold it in place, and gently rub with your fingertips. Lift the paper to see your printed design!

Super Soap

These two prints are negative images, where the shapes were cut out of the soap.

Printing with colored paint on white or colored paper gives your picture a special look.

Use your fingertips to dab colored paints on different parts of your block for exciting results!

Positively Negative

The next time you get pictures developed, ask to see the pieces of negative film. You'll see a reverse image of the people and things in the photographs!

Tempera Silk Screens

Making a Silk Screen

Silk screening is a stencil process using fabric. The cloth is specially prepared so that when paint is pushed through, it prints a design onto paper underneath. Silk screen printing is easy when you use a common embroidery hoop and thin cotton cloth.

Materials needed:

Tempera paint

Embroidery hoop

2 yards (2 meters) of cotton organdy cloth

Masking tape

White glue

Pencil

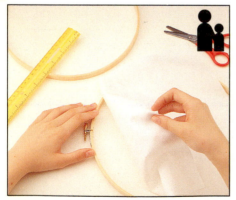

1 To make a hoop screen, cut a piece of cloth a little bigger than the hoop. Take the two rings of the hoop apart and lay the cloth over the bigger hoop.

2 Lay the smaller hoop over the cloth and push it down inside the bigger hoop, catching the cloth in between. Pull the edges of the cloth until it's tight like a drum.

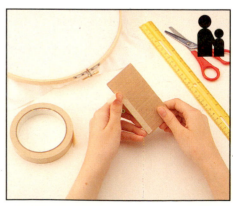

3 Make a squeegee by cutting a 4" by 2" (10 cm by 5 cm) piece of stiff cardboard and wrapping masking tape around one long edge.

Stickers

Construction paper
Notebook paper

Scissors and ruler

Stiff cardboard

Newspaper

Paper Stencils

Cut paper design

Cut Paper Stencil

1 Cut a design in a piece of notebook paper. A snowflake works great—fold the paper and cut little shapes out, then unfold it.

2 Lay the cut paper stencil flat on a piece of construction paper. Set your hoop screen down with the stretched cloth pushing down on the stencil.

3 Pour some paint into the hoop. Gently pull the squeegee across the paint three or four times to spread it all over the cloth, scraping extra paint to the side.

Cut paper abstract

Cut paper picture

Sticker abstract

Sticker picture

Sticker Stencil

4 The paint sticks to the stencil and prints a design on the construction paper underneath! Lift the hoop up—paint, stencil and all—and use it again.

5 When you're done, discard the stencil. Take the cloth out of the hoops and wash it in warm water. Use it to print a different cut paper stencil when it's dry.

6 Put a clean piece of cloth in the hoops. Stick pieces of tape and stickers onto the cloth to make a design. Use your squeegee and paint to print onto paper.

White Glue Stencil

1 Make a hoop screen and prop it up so the cloth doesn't touch the table. Put scrap newspaper underneath.

2 Draw a simple design or picture on the cloth with a pencil. Squeeze glue onto the cloth along the lines of your pencil sketch.

3 Let the glue dry overnight. Use your squeegee to push paint through the cloth onto construction paper underneath.